W9-AWI-296

An American Bird Conservancy Compact Guide

Paul Lehman
Ornithological Editor

The American Bird Conservancy (**ABC**) is a lean, high-output, nonprofit organization practicing conservation by bringing together partners whose expertise and resources are best suited to each task. ABC is the US partner of BirdLife International, the world bird conservation partnership.

ABC supports **Partners in Flight** (**PIF**), an Americas-wide coalition of organizations, agencies, private companies, and individuals implementing a science-based strategy for conserving all American bird species and their habitats. Information about PIF's strategy, called *Flight Plan*, can be obtained from ABC, the National Fish and Wildlife Foundation, or the US Fish and Wildlife Service. PIF's National Coordination is on ABC's staff, and ABC implements the Flight Plan through its Globally Important Bird Area initiative.

ABC's Policy Council is a forum composed of 70 member organizations providing scientific and policy advice to conservationists; exchanging information on emerging bird conservation issues; stimulating a network of support for conservation policies; and directly accomplishing conservation through ABC. Collaboration among council organizations has assisted in the protection of numerous species, including Swainson's hawk, San Clemente loggerhead shrike and Atlantic Coast migratory shorebirds.

ABC members receive *Bird Conservation*, the magazine about PIF and American bird conservation, and *World Birdwatch*, the magazine about bird conservation worldwide.

ALL THE
BACKYARD
BIRDS
E A S T

BY JACK L. GRIGGS

Barn Owl

HarperPerennial
A Division of HarperCollins*Publishers*

Dedicated to Jack L. Griggs Sr.

Designed by Jack L. Griggs & Peg Alrich

Edited by Virginia Croft

Illustrations reformatted by Jack E. Griggs
from the original illustrations published in
All the Birds of North America
by the following artists:

F. P. Bennett p. 29 (bottom); John Dawson pp. 41-47,
49 (top and center), 75, 77; Dale Dyer pp. 79-89; Larry McQueen pp. 61-73;
Hans Peeters pp. 19-25, 31, 33, 49 (bottom), 51-59; Doug Pratt pp. 35-39;
and Andrew Vallely; p. 27, 29 (top).

ALL THE BACKYARD BIRDS: EAST

FIRST EDITION

Library of Congress Cataloging-in-Publication Data
Available upon request.
ISBN 0-06-273631-0
98 99 00 01 02 10 9 8 7 6 5 4 3 2

Contents

HOW TO ATTRACT BIRDS

by
SCOTT EDWARDS

There are four fundamental attractions for birds: food, water, shelter, and a place to raise their young, all of which are easily provided in backyards.

Food is the most basic and obvious bird attraction, and more birds are attracted to black-oil sunflower seeds ("oilers" to bird-feeding veterans) than to any other seed. The black-oil sunflower seeds are smaller compared to the more familiar large striped varieties. Other attractive seeds are thistle seeds, striped sunflower seeds, split peanuts, peanuts in the shell, white proso millet, and various nuts.

It is important to note that not everything labeled "birdseed" is eaten by birds. Many birdseed mixes contain filler products, seeds that add only weight and actually detract from the mix's attractiveness. Grains like milo, oats, wheat, rice, and canary seed, as well as the ambiguous "mixed grain products," are best avoided. Table scraps are not recommended for birds either. Bread crumbs, crackers, and similar foods are just empty calories that offer very little nutrition.

When most people think of bird-feeding, they think first of offering seed. However, only a

minority of the birds that surround us are seed-crushers. Many additional birds can be attracted to your feeding station if you offer suet, fruit, mealworms, or nectar.

Suet is the fat that surrounds beef kidneys. It will attract woodpeckers, chickadees, titmice, nuthatches, and brown creepers. It is also occasionally eaten by catbirds, mockingbirds, orioles, and pine warblers, among others. Suet is very dense and should not be confused with fat trimmings from other beef parts. Plain fat is not as beneficial, has a much higher water content, and will freeze in cold weather.

Suet is not just for winter feeding. Most commercially available suets have been rendered, meaning that they have been boiled repeatedly to remove impurities and to prevent them from going rancid. There is even "summer suet" or suet doughs that are made to survive hot weather without melting.

Suet is best attached directly to the trunk of a large deciduous tree, at least initially. This is where the birds that feed on suet look for their food in the wild.

Fruit like oranges, grapes, and bananas attract orioles and tanagers. Bug-eating birds such

as bluebirds, wrens, and many others readily take mealworms. And, of course, no feeding station would be complete without the presence of nectar for hummingbirds.

The accepted formula for hummingbird nectar is four to five parts water to one part plain table sugar. I don't recommend the use of commercially prepared nectars or the use of coloring. Do not use any artificial sweeteners or honey. It is important to maintain a nectar feeder regularly. Nectar ferments rapidly and can be hazardous to hummingbirds if left out for more than a day or two. Nectar should be changed more often in hot weather.

How to dispense bird food, particularly seed, is an important choice to make. There are three basic designs for seed feeders; the tube feeder, usually made of polycarbonate and designed to hang from a tree or hook; the open platform feeder, which may or may not be covered; and the hopper feeder, basically a platform feeder with a Plexiglas center (the hopper) to hold and dispense seed.

Most tube feeders are designed to dispense black-oil sunflower seeds. Nearly all of the small seed-eaters that perch on tube feeders have such a strong preference for oilers that

using a mixture of seeds is often counter-productive. If you are presently filling your tube feeders with mixed seeds, you have probably witnessed the birds employing a technique called "bill sweeping." By sweeping their beaks from side to side, the birds remove everything but the oilers. And you get to fill your tubes more often.

Some tube feeders have very small ports designed to dispense thistle (technically known as niger) seed. These feeders primarily attract goldfinches.

All tube feeders are designed for small birds. The jays, cardinals, grosbeaks, grackles, and woodpeckers are too big to use them. This is good for the small seed-eaters, which are often bullied off feeders that will accommodate larger birds. But if you can only have one feeder, you should consider a hopper feeder.

Hopper feeders are the most popular type, and a well-designed one will provide enough room to attract a large variety of birds. Both perching birds and ground feeders will visit a hopper feeder with a large landing area. The large seed capacity of the hopper feeder is another attractive feature for the people who have to fill them. Many hopper feeders will hold several pounds of birdseed and don't have to be filled every day. Because of the variety of birds a hopper feeder can attract, it is an excellent place to use a high-quality mixture of seeds.

The platform or fly-through feeder attracts perhaps the widest variety of birds. The open design of these feeders allows birds to come and go from all directions. There is no dispensing mechanism to clog, so you are free to use virtually any food or combination of foods. Use peanuts in the shell if you want regular visits from jays, woodpeckers, and nutcrackers. These feeders are also ideal for serving fruit during the warmer months. I attach suet to my platform feeder to increase visits from woodpeckers, titmice chickadees, and nuthatches.

About four times a year it is a good idea to give your feeders a thorough cleaning. Feeders can get dirty, and wet seed can mold rapidly, making a feeding station unhealthy. Once a season I take down all my feeders over the course of a few days, hose them, soak them in a strong solution of white vinegar, and scrub them with a long-handled brush designed for feeder cleaning. I use vinegar, not bleach, because of the toxicity of chlorine and the fact that it can cloud tube feeders. Regular cleaning will help insure a healthy feeding station in your yard.

All birds must drink and bathe, so the inclusion of a birdbath with a dripper or mister will greatly enhance the attractiveness of your backyard habitat to birds, as can a recirculating pond. Drippers and misters are accessories that attach to your outside water source and provide fresh, moving water for birds. Most drippers utilize a low-flow system that constantly drips water into your water feature.

Misters spray the area around your water feature with a fine mist. They are especially effective if your water feature is surrounded by foliage. While some birds hesitate to immerse themselves, they may "leaf-bathe," an action that has them rubbing their feathers against wet leaves. Misters are also very attractive to hummingbirds, which love to fly around in the mist these accessories create.

Nest boxes are used by many birds that nest in cavities (tree hollows). Bluebirds, nuthatches, wrens, and woodpeckers are a few of the species that will accept your hospitality if you erect the appropriate nest box. Some lucky people are even able to attract screech-owls!

Nest boxes should be made of untreated, unpainted wood. Red cedar or white pine 3/4 to 1 inch thick is preferable. Preservative,

paints, or stains are unnecessary and may
actually be harmful. The exact dimensions
of the box vary depending on which bird you
are attempting to attract. This information is
readily available at any good library or nature
center. Nest boxes must be maintained
regularly and cleaned of nesting debris after
each brood fledges. Keep a logbook on the
progress of the birds using your nest boxes,
especially one with bluebirds in it. All nest
inspections should stop approximately ten
days after the eggs hatch, or the nestlings
may fledge prematurely.

Habitat enhancement is really the key to
attracting the most interesting birds to your
backyard. Successfully attracting a wide variety
and number of birds to your backyard entails
more than just supplying feeders, seed, a pond,
or nest boxes, however. I have dozens of different feeders at my station, but there is more bird
activity per square foot in my two brush piles
(conglomerations of limbs, branches, and old
Christmas trees) than anywhere else in my yard.

Juncos, towhees, and native sparrows such as
the white-throated nest and feed in the brush
piles, and all the little songbirds seek cover
there when a Cooper's or sharp-shinned hawk
comes looking for an easy meal. If a brush pile
is impractical, consider letting a small section of

your backyard go wild. Don't mow, don't prune, just let it grow and watch the birds show up!

Add fruit-bearing trees to your backyard habitat (mountain ash, hackberry, mulberry, and sassafras, for example) and you can attract waxwings, mockingbirds, warblers, catbirds, and bluebirds. Coniferous trees and shrubs such as juniper and holly are wonderful bird attractions and provide cover as well as food.

You can find assistance in improving your backyard habitat at your local nature center and at some of the better wild bird supply stores. Don't be discouraged if your first improvements don't get immediate results. Over time your backyard can become an oasis for birds.

Keep a good pair of binoculars on your windowsill next to this guide to identify the rarer birds your feeder attracts. Binoculars for birding should be 7 or 8 power, bright, sharp, and easy to hold. Stay away from cute gadgets like zooms, perma- or insta-focus, and strange-colored lenses. If you wear eyeglasses, you should be able to leave them on while using your binoculars. The wider your binoculars' field of vision (a salesperson can explain how this is measured) the easier they will be to use.

13

HOW TO LOOK AT A BIRD

The way birds feed and their adaptations for feeding are the most important points to recognize in identifying and understanding a bird. For the beginner, the color and pattern of an unknown bird can be so striking that important points of shape and behavior go unnoticed. But feeding adaptations, especially bill shape, best reveal a bird's role in nature — its truest identity.

Owls, hawks, doves, woodpeckers, and many other birds are easily recognized by shape and behavior. Songbirds are more confusing. If you don't immediately recognize a songbird as a sparrow, a wren, or a warbler, for example, look at its bill shape. Is it a seed-crusher or a bug-eater? Seed-crushers have strong, conical bills for cracking seeds. The shape of a bug-eater's bill varies with the way it catches bugs.

conical bill

Most bug-eaters have slender, straight bills used to probe in trees, brush, ground litter, and rock crevices. A few have curved bills for specialized probing. And some, the flycatcher group, have broad-based, flat bills. Flycatchers catch bugs in midair, and their broad bills improve their chances of success.

straight bill

curved bill

If bill shape can't be seen, a bird's feeding behavior is often just as revealing. Sparrows

flycatching bill

don't flit among the branches of a tree searching for bugs, and warblers won't be seen on the ground picking at seeds.

Knowing its bill shape or feeding behavior reduces the possible identities of an unknown bird. Plumage marks can then be used to identify all the backyard species.

Underside of tail showing tail spots and undertail coverts.

Most names used to describe parts of a bird are predictable — back, crown, throat, etc. Three names that might not be immediately understood are rump, undertail coverts, and wing bars. The rump is at the base of the tail, topside; undertail coverts cover the base of the tail, bottomside. Wing bars are formed by the contrasting tips (often white) of the feathers that help cover the wing when it is folded.

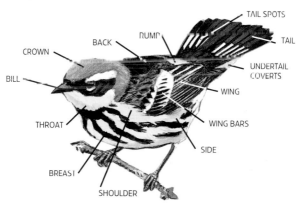

TAIL SPOTS
BACK
RUMP
TAIL
CROWN
UNDERTAIL COVERTS
BILL
WING
THROAT
WING BARS
SIDE
BREAST
SHOULDER

HOW TO READ THE MAPS

ange maps provide a simplified picture of a species' distribution. They indicate the birds that can be expected in any local region. Birds are not evenly distributed over their ranges. They require suitable habitat (no seeds, no sparrows) and are typically scarcest at their range limits. Some birds are numerous but not commonly seen because they are secretive.

Weather and food availability affect bird distribution in winter. Some birds regularly retreat south to escape winter weather. Others leave their northern ranges only occasionally. Some whose resident population slowly creeps northward in mild winters may perish if their newly occupied range is hit by a hard winter.

MAP KEY

SUMMER OR
NESTING

WINTER

ALL YEAR

MIGRATION
(spring & fall)

HOW THE BIRDS ARE ORGANIZED

EASTERN SCREECH-OWL

COMMON NIGHTHAWK

BARN OWL

The great horned owl might be heard from backyards. It gives a deep *hoo, hoo-hoo, hoo, hoo* or similar five- or six-note call.

Although seldom seen because they hunt in the evenings and at night, some owls are surprisingly common near houses and farms. **Eastern screech-owls** are often found in suburban woodlots or parks, where their calls — a long mournful whinny or a long low trill — can be heard. They are the only small owl in the East with ear tufts, or "horns." Sometimes the ear tufts are held flat, however, and are not visible. Screech-owls can be gray, brown, or a rusty red.

Barn owls are still numerous in the Southeast, but the northern population is seriously declining with loss of habitat and the great number of road kills. The **barn owl** is often recognized by its heart-shaped face. Its pale body and long legs are also good marks. Barn owls screech, and screech-owls give a whistling tone, proving that bird names are often misleading.

Nighthawks (another misleading name; they are not hawks) sweep through the skies feeding like swifts or swallows. They are locally common over woodlands and some towns and cities at dusk and dawn, but have declined markedly in the East in the last 25 years. Note the **nighthawk's** white wing patch and listen for its nasal *peent* flight call.

Eastern Screech-owl

young

gray form

red form

Common Nighthawk

Barn Owl

VULTURES

Large black birds with unfeathered heads seen tugging at a piece of road kill are easily recognized as vultures – the "buzzards" of the old West. Adult **turkey vultures** are the ones with red heads. Young turkey vultures are dark-headed, however, and can be mistaken for black vultures.

Dark-headed birds are best identified by shape, especially tail length. The **black vulture** is more compact and has a short tail that barely extends beyond the folded wing of a standing bird. Turkey vultures, young and old, are rangier birds with a longer tail.

When not feeding, vultures are usually seen soaring high overhead in search of carrion. Even at a great distance, they can often be recognized by their flight style and the contrasting pattern of pale and dark on their underwing. Only the outer wing feathers of the black vulture's wing are pale. Turkey vultures often tip a bit from side to side as they soar and usually hold their wings above horizontal in a shallow V. Black vultures soar on flat wings and often give a series of quick, shallow flaps.

Black vultures are less common than turkey vultures but are slowly expanding their range in the Northeast.

TURKEY VULTURE

BLACK VULTURE

Vultures typically soar on thermals and updrafts. Because black vultures have shorter wings, they don't soar as buoyantly as turkey vultures. Black vultures have to flap a bit more and might stay grounded on a day that a turkey vulture could soar.

Turkey Vulture

black vulture

turkey vulture

black vulture

Black Vulture

HAWKS

The kestrel and red-tailed hawk are not likely to be seen in backyards, but they are common along roads and in parks. The red-tailed hawk is often seen soaring. A Kestrel hunts from a perch, typically a wire or pole overlooking a vacant lot or other open area. It will often return to the same perch daily if it is successful in capturing the mice, large insects, or small birds that are its prey. Kestrels often hover over suspected prey.

KESTREL

RED-TAILED HAWK

The **kestrel** is identified by its size, only 10 to 12 inches long, and two black face streaks contrasting with white cheeks and throat. Males are smaller than females, and the blue on the male's wings contrasts with the red on its back and tail. There is no such contrast in the upperparts of the female, which are an even red with heavy dark barring.

The local breeding population of peregrine falcons in the East was largely lost to pesticide sprays in the mid-1900s.

Peregrines have been reintroduced in many eastern cities. They roost and nest on bridges and high buildings. Pigeons are their preferred meal.

The red-tailed hawk seen soaring over your backyard is not likely to harass birds at your feeder like the hawks on the following pages do. Nearly all adult eastern **red-tailed hawks** have a red tail (pink from below) and dark streaks on the belly that often form a band. Young birds have brownish tails with many narrow dark bands. The dark bars along the leading edge of the underwing are good marks for identifying soaring birds.

Kestrel

young

eastern

western

Red-tailed Hawk

eastern

young

HAWKS

COOPER'S HAWK

SHARP-SHINNED HAWK

Young hawks of some larger species (buteos) may be confused with a young Cooper's, but they don't attack at backyard feeders as a Cooper's does. And Cooper's hawk seldom sits openly on roadside perches as buteos do.

Cooper's and sharp-shinned hawks are the birds of prey known for attacking songbirds at backyard bird feeders and sometimes colliding with picture windows. They seldom perch openly or soar overhead like the hawks described on the previous pages. Instead, they typically lurk in foliage until prey appears and then, with a sprinter's explosive burst, ambush the unsuspecting dinner.

Except in size, the two species are nearly identical. Both **Cooper's** and the **sharp-shinned** have long tails with distinctive broad dark and pale bands. Adults are blue-gray above with rusty barring below. Young birds are brown above and have brown streaking on their underparts.

Size differences between Cooper's and the sharp-shinned are sometimes hard to judge. A small male sharpie (about 12 inches long) can be distinguished from a large female Cooper's (about 18 inches), but most individuals are somewhere in between.

Small differences in their tails are the best marks separating the two species but are very difficult to see. The tip of a Cooper's tail is round and banded white. The sharpie's tail has squarer corners and a narrow gray terminal band.

Typical variations in
sharp-shinned hawk's tail

young
sharp-shinned

young Cooper's

Cooper's

young

sharp-shinned

young

adults shown in typical
flight; young birds soaring

Cooper's Hawk

young

**Sharp-shinned
Hawk**

young

SWALLOWS

TREE SWALLOW

PURPLE MARTIN

BARN SWALLOW

Two other swallows are brown above and white below like young tree swallows. The bank swallow has a brown breast band; the rough-winged, a dirty-brown throat and upper breast.

Swallows are sleek and speedy aerialists that spend most of their day capturing bugs in flight. Because flying insects abound near water, swallows often fly over water. When not feeding, they can be seen together, side by side, on a wire by the dozens. Tree swallows nest in boxes; martins use communal nest boxes. Barn swallows commonly make cup-shaped mud nests under eaves.

It isn't easy to get a good look at a flying swallow, but most can be identified at a glance if you know what to look for. The **tree swallow** is the only eastern swallow that is white below and glossy blue-green above. Young birds are brown above. Note that the tree swallow doesn't have a "swallowtail."

The **barn swallow** is the swallow with the forked tail shape that has become a graphic symbol of speed and grace. The upperparts are a deep blue on all birds, but the orange-buff underparts can be paler on young birds. Also, the tail streamers of young birds are often shorter than the adults'.

The **purple martin** is our largest swallow, and the only species in which the sexes differ strongly. The male is an even blue–black. Females are duller above and gray below with a gray collar.

Tree Swallow

Purple Martin

young

♂

♀

Barn Swallow

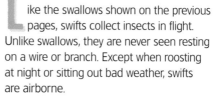

SWIFT AND HUMMINGBIRD

CHIMNEY SWIFT

RUBY-THROATED HUMMINGBIRD

Hummingbird feeders in the South are attracting increasing numbers of vagrant western and Mexican hummers in fall and over the winter.

Chimney swifts once roosted in hollow trees in the original eastern forest. Now they primarily use chimneys.

Like the swallows shown on the previous pages, swifts collect insects in flight. Unlike swallows, they are never seen resting on a wire or branch. Except when roosting at night or sitting out bad weather, swifts are airborne.

The only eastern swift, the **chimney swift,** is a dark bird with a pale throat that flies rapidly and erratically. The flight style itself is the best mark distinguishing it from swallows. Rapid, shallow wing beats create a unique twinkling effect that, once seen, is easily noted. The swift can seem to flap its wings alternately. Swallows fly more gracefully.

The **ruby-throated hummingbird** is the only hummer that occurs throughout the East. It is the male that has the ruby throat, which most often appears flat black. Only when light is reflected at a favorable angle can the flash of ruby red be seen. Female hummers lack the male's brilliant throat feathers, although some may sport a few dots of red. Tail shapes of male and female ruby-throats are also distinctively different.

Hummingbirds are usually seen singly or in small numbers in spring, but larger numbers may congregate at a backyard feeder in late summer or early fall.

Chimney Swift

Ruby-throated
Hummingbird

♀

♂

GAMEBIRDS

Gamebirds have learned to be very cautious and to stay hidden to protect themselves. They are prey to many wild animals, as well as humans. Only a few gamebirds are found on cultivated land or in areas near people.

The eastern gamebirds that live closest to humans are the bobwhite and the ring-necked pheasant. Bobwhites are common in fields and hedgerows and will even venture into rural backyards. Pheasants are common in farmlands, but local populations regularly plummet and rebound.

Bobwhites are a species of quail. They live in coveys (small flocks) most of the time. When nesting and raising young, they are paired. Identifying a **bobwhite** is usually just a matter of recognizing its call, a whistled *bob-white!* Males are reddish brown with a white throat and eyebrow. Females are duller and have a buff throat and eyebrow.

Pheasants were introduced from Asia and have a number of color variations. Some males have green bodies; others have white wings; some lack the neck ring. All males have a red eye patch. The most common form is illustrated. Both sexes have distinctive long pointed tails.

BOBWHITE

RING-NECKED PHEASANT

Wild turkeys were once numerous in open woodlands of the South and East, then were hunted to scarcity in most areas. Now they are managed as a gamebird in all 48 adjacent states.

30

Bobwhite

♀ ♂

Ring-necked Pheasant

♀ ♂

DOVES

Eurasian collared-doves are now common in some southern cities. They have a black collar like a ringed turtle-dove (a cage bird), but give a *coo-coo-coo* instead of the turtle-dove's bubbling call.

Doves (or pigeons — there is no difference) can be depended on to show up at backyard feeders. They have very short legs and walk on the ground like game-birds rather than hopping along like most birds. As they walk, they bob their heads back and forth in a characteristic fashion.

The **common ground-dove** was once common along the Gulf of Mexico. Large numbers remain only in Florida. Smaller than the mourning or rock dove, it has a scaled breast and flashes rusty red in its wings when it flies.

Mourning doves and rock doves are widespread and abundant. **Mourning doves** are the ones with long pointed tails. Doves are a popular symbol for peace, but at a feeder, mourning doves can be quite aggressive among themselves. A mournful call, *woo-oó-oo, oo, oo, oo,* is given in spring and summer by unmated males.

Rock dove is the formal name for the well-known pigeon of cities and farms. It originally nested on cliffs. Pigeons have colonized most of the world in the company of man. The many color variations seen are the result of interbreeding with exotic domesticated strains. The ancestral form is shown in the foreground.

32

Common Ground-dove

♂

♀

Mourning Dove

Rock Dove

WOODPECKERS

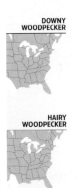

DOWNY
WOODPECKER

HAIRY
WOODPECKER

The pileated wood-
pecker is sometimes
seen in mature trees
in parks or woodlots.
It is a large, mostly
black bird the size
of a crow, with a
pointed, flaming red
crest and white wing
patches.

The most common woodpecker in eastern backyards is the downy. It is also the smallest, just 7 inches long. The hairy woodpecker has virtually the identical plumage pattern but is 2 inches larger. It is a frequent visitor to suet feeders.

The size difference is easy to recognize when the two species are seen side by side, but can be hard to judge when the birds are seen separately. The best mark is the bill length. The **hairy woodpecker** has a much larger bill — nearly as long as its head. The **downy woodpecker's** bill extends only about half its head length.

Males of both species have a bright red patch on the back of their crowns that is lacking in females. Young birds (both sexes) also show a patch of red on their heads, but the color is more diffuse and is located on the center or forepart of the crown rather than on the rear.

There is a very small plumage difference that can be noted on birds at close range. The white outer tail feathers on the hairy woodpecker are unmarked, while those on the downy woodpecker have two or more black bars.

young

hairy

Downy
Woodpecker

♀

♂

Hairy
Woodpecker

♀

♂

WOODPECKERS

RED-BELLIED WOODPECKER

YELLOW-SHAFTED FLICKER

The red-bellied woodpecker is sometimes mistakenly called a red-headed woodpecker.

There is a red-headed woodpecker, and it was once common. The adult has a completely red head and neck. It has become scarce as a result of competition for nest holes with starlings.

Several different woodpeckers show up regularly in backyards, particularly at suet feeders. The red-bellied woodpecker on these pages and the hairy and downy woodpeckers on the previous pages are the most commonly seen.

The yellow-shafted flicker (a woodpecker) is much rarer at suet feeders. It is usually seen on the ground in parks or other open short-grass areas feeding on ants, its favorite meal. Flickers also gather insects from trees like other woodpeckers, but because they often feed on the ground, they are sometimes not recognized as woodpeckers.

The typical view of a **yellow-shafted flicker** is of a white-rumped bird rising in flight from the ground and flying directly away, flashing yellow in the underwing. Seen closer, the flicker has strikingly patterned plumage. The male has a black mustache mark lacking in females.

Red-bellied woodpeckers do have a red belly, but it is a small pale red blush that isn't a good field mark. The black-and-white barred back, or "ladder-back," is a better mark. The red patch on the nape and hind neck of the female continues over the crown and forehead on the male.

red-headed woodpecker

♂

♀
Red-bellied
Woodpecker

Yellow-shafted
Flicker

♂ ♀

NUTHATCHES AND CREEPER

WHITE-BREASTED
NUTHATCH

RED-BREASTED
NUTHATCH

BROWN CREEPER

The black-and-white
warbler (p. 68)
behaves a lot like a
nuthatch, picking
insects from limbs
and trunks of trees.

Not all birds seen climbing a tree trunk are woodpeckers. Nuthatches and the brown creeper also make a living on the insects and larvae hidden in a tree's bark. Nuthatches are the only tree-climbers so agile that they can creep down a tree. Presumably they find morsels that upward-climbers miss. They also forage for insects at the tips of small branches and take seeds from pine cones.

The **white-breasted nuthatch** is the most common nuthatch at most feeders. It is dark above and white below with an inconspicuous wash of rusty red on its flanks. Females are the same as males, except some are noticeably grayer on the crown.

Red-breasted nuthatches prefer conifers and are common only in the northern portion of the eastern US. They are smaller and even bolder than the white-breasted. Note the rusty red underparts and black eyestripe. Females are duller than males.

The **brown creeper** is often overlooked. It can appear on the trunk of any tree, especially mature ones, and blends into the background of bark. It spirals up a tree trunk and is often first noticed flying from one tree to the base of another.

White-breasted
Nuthatch

♀

Red-
breasted
Nuthatch

♂

Brown Creeper

**EASTERN
KINGBIRD**

CEDAR WAXWING

In coastal Florida, especially the Keys, the gray kingbird can often be seen perched on utility wires. As its name suggests, it is grayer above than the eastern kingbird. It also lacks the white tip to its notched tail and has a narrow black mask.

Waxwings wander in flocks of up to a hundred birds or so except when nesting. They keep in close contact, giving a pleasing high-pitched, lisping call. A flock of these sleek birds will often sit awhile in the top of a tall tree before flying down to feed on fruit or berries. They also catch insects, flycatcher fashion, in summer.

The small dots of red on the wings are the source of the waxwing's name. They suggest the wax once used for sealing documents. The crest, narrow dark mask, and yellow tail tip are the easiest marks for identifying the **cedar waxwing.** It is the only eastern bird with a yellow-tipped tail, and the **eastern kingbird** is the only one with a white-tipped tail.

The eastern kingbird is a flycatcher like the eastern phoebe and great crested flycatcher shown on the next pages. All wait patiently for an insect to pass their perch. After catching it on the wing, the flycatcher often returns to the same perch to repeat the process.

The kingbird is particularly conspicuous, preferring a high perch in an open area from which to watch for flying insects. Its noisy, aggressive behavior also draws attention. Other birds or people that come too near a nest are subject to attack.

Eastern Kingbird

Cedar Waxwing

young

FLYCATCHERS

One of the most familiar flycatchers, the eastern phoebe has adapted well to civilization and frequently nests under eaves or bridges, or on any flat surface protected by an overhang. Barns are especially popular nest sites because of the abundance of flying insects. Like many other songbirds, phoebes often return each spring to the same nest site.

There are other small flycatchers (see sidebar) resembling a phoebe — dark above, pale below — but only the **eastern phoebe** pumps its tail downward. The name comes from its call, a forceful *fee-bee,* alternately rising and falling in pitch and given repeatedly.

The great crested flycatcher is common in forests and orchards and ventures to the shade trees of residential areas. Like the eastern kingbird shown on the previous page, it can be noisy and aggressive. The **great crested flycatcher's** yellow belly is a good mark, but the best mark is often the rusty red flash in the wings and tail of the bird as it flies.

All flycatchers are migrants, heading south when summer ends. Phoebes are the hardiest, the only flycatcher wintering in the eastern US, except for a few great crested flycatchers that remain in South Florida.

EASTERN PHOEBE

GREAT CRESTED FLYCATCHER

Most often confused with the phoebe are the eastern wood-pewee and the empidonax flycatchers.

The empidonax are a closely related group of flycatchers that have white wing bars and eye rings. Pewees have wing bars but no eye rings.

Eastern Phoebe

young

Great Crested
Flycatcher

BROWN THRASHER

HOUSE WREN

CAROLINA WREN

Winter wrens are scarce but could show up in a backyard brush pile. They are a smaller version of the house wren with an even stubbier tail and a buff eyebrow.

The thrashers and wrens have curved bills that they use to probe for bugs. Thrashers use their bills to rake the soil and leaf litter under shrubs and bushes for insects. Because they are shy and often hidden, thrashers are frequently heard thrashing through the debris under a bush before they are seen. When surprised, they usually fly straight and low into a nearby bush.

The **brown thrasher** is sometimes confused with the wood thrush (p. 56). Both birds are rusty brown above and spotted below, but the brown thrasher has a curved bill and a longer tail. Also, its spots form streaks.

Wrens are not likely to be confused with other birds, even if their slightly curved bill is not noticed. No other small brown bird has similar fine barring on its wings and tail, and none cock their tail or scold so expressively. The **Carolina wren's** white eyebrow and buff underparts are the easiest marks separating it from the house wren. There is little to distinguish the mousy little **house wren** other than its wren shape and fine barring.

The Carolina and the house wrens are both common around houses. In the area above the dotted line on the map, the Carolina wren disappears after particularly hard winters.

Brown Thrasher

wood thrush
p. 56

House Wren

Carolina Wren

GRACKLE AND CROWS

COMMON GRACKLE

AMERICAN CROW

FISH CROW

Boat-tailed grackles inhabit coastal marshes and Florida. Great-tailed grackles inhabit western Gulf states. Males of both species are half again as big as common grackles.

Most people with backyard feeders would consider grackles all too common. They feed in open areas and are opportunists that will eat grains, insects, or almost anything else they can subdue. The conversion of forest to open land throughout the East has allowed them to proliferate.

The **common grackle** has a longer tail than similar black birds seen near suburbs and farms. The tails of males in summer are distinctively wedge shaped, and in flight the central feathers are often depressed, creating a "keel" shape rather than a flat surface.

Adult male grackles have a purple or bronze sheen to their black plumage. Females show less sheen and only on the head, breast, and upper back. Young birds are a dull brown with brown, not yellow, eyes.

Crows and their larger relatives, ravens, are considered the most intelligent birds. Like grackles, they have benefitted from fields replacing forest. Scientists recognize two species in the East, the **fish crow** and the **American crow.** Fish crows are numerous in coastal marshes. They average a bit smaller than American crows, but the only reliable mark is their call, a two-noted nasal *eh-eh* rather than the familiar *caw.*

46

young

♀

♂

Common Grackle

American and Fish Crows

MOCKINGBIRD, JAY, BLACKBIRD

BLUE JAY

MOCKINGBIRD

RED–WINGED BLACKBIRD

The loggerhead shrike can be found some-times on roadside fences. The shrike is like a mocker but has a shorter bill, a black mask, and a different white wing patch.

A common and familiar bird, especially in the South, the mockingbird will perch conspicuously on a wire, limb, or often a TV antenna and serenade tirelessly throughout the year, even into the night. It is a famous mimic and will repeat grating, mechanical sounds as readily as the songs of other birds. The **mockingbird** is a slim gray bird with a long tail that it often holds erect. The white in its wings is a prominent mark when it flies.

Noisy and colorful, the **blue jay** is familiar to backyard birders. It dominates at a feeder and often fills its crop (a storage pouch in the throat) with sunflower seeds before flying off. It stores the seeds in the woods for winter or in case you forget to refill your feeder.

Red-winged blackbirds are widely known by the male's orange–red shoulder patches, although often only the yellowish lower border is visible when the bird is at rest. The female looks like a big streaked sparrow, sometimes with a bit of red blush on the face or shoulder. She is much scarcer around feeders than the male. Young birds look like females. The young male gradually acquires his adult plumage by fall of his second year.

48

Blue Jay

Mockingbird

mockingbird

loggerhead shrike

Red-winged
Blackbird

♂

♀

STARLING AND COWBIRD

The starling and cowbird are the villains among birds. Neither is native to the East, and both have raised havoc with native birds as their numbers have multiplied.

Originally introduced from Europe, the starling nests in cavities and has displaced native cavity nesters such as the purple martin (p. 26), the red-headed woodpecker and the eastern bluebird (p. 58).

The **starling's** plumage varies by season from spotted to glossy black. The birds have very short tails and long pointed bills. **The brown-headed cowbird's** best mark is its short conical bill. Males are black with a dark brown head; females, a dull gray-brown. Cowbirds are illustrated here rather than with the other conically billed birds because they are easily confused with blackbirds and starlings.

Cowbirds were originally birds of the Great Plains and were then known as "buffalo birds." They spread across the East when the original forest was felled. Cowbirds are nest parasites. They lay an egg in other birds' nests, and the host birds raise the cowbird chick, usually at the expense of their own young. Since mankind is responsible for the spread of the cowbird and the introduction of the starling, perhaps we are the villains.

STARLING

BROWN-HEADED COWBIRD

Another cowbird, the shiny cowbird from the Caribbean, is invading the East. It reached Florida in 1985 and is spreading throughout the state but is still rare.

Male shiny cowbirds are black with a violet gloss; females are similar to the brown-headed female.

fall

young

Starling

spring

molting young ♂ in fall

Brown-headed Cowbird

♀

♂

ORIOLES

Adult male orioles are unmistakable, but females and young birds can be confusing. Female **orchard orioles** are olive green above and yellow to yellow-green below with two white wing bars. They lack the orange tones of the female Baltimore oriole and are noticeably smaller.

Young orchard orioles in their first summer and fall look very much like the female. The young males take two years to become adult, and the yearling male has a black chin and throat that distinguishes it from females and younger birds.

Female and young **Baltimore orioles** are particularly variable. Some females can show a lot of black on the head or throat (similar to the male) and have warm orange tones below. Other females, particularly young birds, can be yellowish and plain. Yearling males show orange and black splotches.

Female orioles can be confused with the female tanager shown on the next pages, as well as with each other. Note, however, that the female tanager lacks wing bars and has a distinctively shaped "swollen" bill.

Orioles often build their hanging, pendant-shaped nests in large shade trees.

ORCHARD ORIOLE

BALTIMORE ORIOLE

Orioles, meadow-larks, and blackbirds are all closely related, as can be seen by the bill shape in particular. All belong to a family known as icterids.

Orioles are fond of fruit and will feed on a halved orange or from a hummingbird-style nectar feeder.

young ♂

Orchard Oriole

♀

♂

Baltimore Oriole

♀

♂

young ♂

TANAGER AND MEADOWLARK

SCARLET TANAGER

EASTERN MEADOWLARK

There are two species of meadowlarks. The eastern meadowlark is the most common in the East, but western meadowlarks extend as far east as the Great Lakes.

Western meadowlarks look the same but have a different song, a bubbling, flute-like melody.

Scarlet tanagers are not common in residential areas, but they are regular spring migrants and summer visitors in shade trees. More aren't seen because they are relatively slow-moving birds that often stay hidden in the canopy of mature trees.

Scarlet tanagers are best located by their song and call. The song suggests a robin's whistled phrases but is distinctively hoarser. The call is also hoarse, a two-noted *chip-burr.*

By fall, males begin molting to a yellowish green plumage like the female's, but the wings and tail remain black. Patchy males can be seen before the birds begin fall migration.

From a perch on a rural fence post or wire, the **eastern meadowlark** often sings its familiar *see-you, see-yeer* song. It is almost as well known for its song as for its bright yellow breast with a black V. It flies with quail-like rapid strokes interrupted by short glides. The white outer tail feathers are often fanned when it glides.

Meadowlarks are seriously declining in the disappearing fields and meadows of the Northeast. They remain common only in their southern range. In fall and winter, they are often in flocks.

spring ♂

Scarlet Tanager

fall molting ♂

♀

Eastern Meadowlark

winter

summer

WOOD THRUSH AND ROBIN

WOOD THRUSH

ROBIN

The only spotted thrush to be seen in winter is the hermit thrush. It might be encountered in a wooded park, especially in the Southeast. It has a reddish tail (which it often pumps) contrasting with a browner back.

Both the wood thrush and the robin are backyard birds. The robin is seen in the open, sunny part of the yard, while the wood thrush prefers shadows and cover. Robins vastly outnumber wood thrushes.

There are several spotted thrushes in addition to the wood thrush that migrate to North America to nest. All are birds of the forest floor and all look much alike, gray-brown to reddish brown above and white below with breast spots. Wood thrushes are the only ones to adapt to backyards, but others might show up during migration.

The bold spotting is a good mark for the **wood thrush,** but the best mark is the contrast of the rusty head and back with the browner rump and tail.

One of the first birds every child learns to recognize is the **robin.** But how many people ever grow up to notice that female robins are distinctively duller above and paler orange below than males? Young birds have spotted breasts like the thrushes, and in fact, robins are thrushes.

The thrushes are accomplished singers. Their distinctive whistled flute-like notes are given in short phrases and carry well.

56

young

Wood Thrush

young

♂

Robin

BLUEBIRD AND CATBIRD

EASTERN BLUEBIRD

CATBIRD

Like robins, bluebirds are a member of the thrush family. They primarily catch prey on the ground like other thrushes, but bluebirds often sit on a fence or low wire to spot their prey.

In many localities, bluebirds depend upon nest boxes. Where nest boxes are provided, they are likely to be common. They once nested wherever there were scattered trees with holes suitable for nesting. Competition for these sites with two introduced species, the starling (p. 50) and the house sparrow (p. 82), have made bluebirds increasingly dependent on nest boxes. And tree swallows (p. 26) compete with them for the nest boxes.

The female **eastern bluebird** is much paler than the impressive male, with bright blue only in the wings and tail. The blue is palest in young birds, which also have spotting on their backs and breasts. Family groups are often seen together throughout the summer. They prefer open habitat with scattered trees. Orchards are a particular favorite.

The catbird is a skulker, much more common in the bushes and thickets of backyards and parks than many bird-watchers suspect. It is closely related to the mockingbird and sings a similar jumble of mimicked sounds and odd notes. Its name comes from a cat-like mewing that it often makes.

The only distinctive marks on the plain gray **catbird** are the rusty patch under the tail, which is hard to see, and the black cap.

young

♀

Eastern Bluebird

♂

Catbird

VIREOS

**BLUE-HEADED
VIREO**

**RED-EYED
VIREO**

**WARBLING
VIREO**

Vireos are often confused with warblers, but a vireo's bill is heavier, more swollen, and vireos feed lethargically.

Although one of the most abundant birds in the East, the red-eyed vireo is not commonly seen. It is hidden in foliage high in trees, from forests to woodlands to backyards. Compared to most small birds, it moves slowly and deliberately as it picks insects from the foliage.

All the vireos forage much like the red-eyed, and all can often be heard singing as they feed. Each vireo states a phrase and then repeats it or a slight variation monotonously, with short pauses in between.

The **red-eyed vireo** runs several notes together, as a robin does, with an inflection up or down at the end of its phrase. The **warbling vireo** has a dozen or more clear notes in its rambling phrase. The **blue-headed** vireo gives a short phrase like the red-eyed, but it is richer, sweeter, usually given more slowly and with longer pauses.

Eye markings and wing bars are the best way to separate vireos visually. The blue-headed has spectacles; the warbling and red-eyed vireos have distinctive eyebrows. All can show pale yellow sides, but only the blue-headed vireo has wing bars. And don't look for red in the eye of the red-eyed; it's hard to see except in good light. The eye usually looks dark.

Blue-headed Vireo

Red-eyed Vireo

Warbling Vireo

yellow
extreme

WARBLERS

CHESTNUT-SIDED WARBLER

Two other warblers in the East have yellow rumps, the magnolia and the Cape May warblers.

The magnolia warbler is described on the next pages. The male Cape May warbler has a red patch around its eye. It is usually seen in ornamental spruce or pine.

Thirty-seven different kinds of warblers — each more beautiful than the other — nest in or migrate through eastern North America. Almost any of them might choose your backyard for a brief layover. The myrtle warbler is one of the most likely visitors; the chestnut-sided warbler is more likely to be seen in an overgrown pasture or a park.

To identify any warbler, begin by noting whether or not it shows yellow and whether or not it has wing bars. If you can get these two marks first and then note any other prominent features, you will have the best chance of success.

Both the **myrtle** and the **chestnut-sided warbler** show yellow and have wing bars. The chestnut-colored side stripe is an obvious mark for male chestnut-sided warblers. It can be absent on young birds seen in fall. Their best mark is the distinctive lime green upperparts and yellow wing bars.

The myrtle warbler has a yellow rump. There is also a distinctive patch of yellow on the side near the shoulder, although it is sometimes faint on young birds in fall. The myrtle is the most abundant eastern warbler in winter, when it feeds heavily on the myrtle berries from which it gets its name.

young

♀

spring ♂

Myrtle Warbler

Chestnut-sided Warbler

spring ♂

young

spring ♀

WARBLERS

BLACK-THROATED GREEN WARBLER

MAGNOLIA WARBLER

Like the warblers shown on the previous pages, the black-throated green and the magnolia warbler show yellow and have distinctive wing bars. Both are numerous and could well appear in the trees or bushes of your backyard during migration. They are even more likely to be seen in a woodland park.

These warblers are also good examples of the typical variations in a warbler's plumage. In most warblers, the boldness of their colors varies with sex, season, age, or all three, but the pattern remains similar. There are a few species, however, in which male and female or spring and fall birds look distinctly different.

Black-throated green warblers don't always have a black throat. The throat is a good mark in adult males and most females, but young birds in fall have white throats. The best mark is the yellow face bordered on the crown and neck with olive green.

Magnolia warblers retain the large band of white in their tail in all plumages. When the tail is half spread, the white becomes an easy mark. The black mask and breast streaks are obvious on spring birds, but in fall, the black mask is gone and the black breast streaks and throat band are replaced by vague grayish markings in many birds.

Few warblers actually warble. Their songs tend to be high-pitched notes and trills. A warbling song is most likely given by a vireo or finch.

Black-throated Green Warbler

♀

young

♂

♀

young

Magnolia
Warbler

spring ♂

WARLERS

The yellowthroat and yellow warbler show yellow but do not have wing bars, as the four warblers shown on the previous pages do. The yellow warbler can have narrow yellow wing bars, but they are generally lost in the overall yellow of the bird.

The male **common yellowthroat** is recognized by its black mask. Females and young birds are more difficult to identify. First, note the yellow and the lack of wing bars. There is yellow on the throat and under the rump, but the belly is brownish gray. The absence of yellow on the belly is the most distinctive mark. The brown cheek is also a useful mark. Yellow extends onto the cheek of most warblers with yellow underparts.

Both of these warblers are common. They forage in shrubs and thickets, and a few are likely to visit backyard bushes or the lower branches of shade trees. If your backyard borders a wetland, you are especially likely to see these birds regularly.

Most **yellow warblers** are bright yellow, and males have red breast streaks. Young birds can be confusing. Look for the beady dark eye and the yellow edges on their wing feathers, which give the wings a striped effect. In flight, the yellow tail spots are visible.

YELLOW WARBLER

COMMON YELLOWTHROAT

Only the prothonotary and the blue-winged warbler are as bright yellow as the yellow warbler.

Prothonotaries are so bright that the males almost glow. The wings and tail, however, are blue-gray. The blue-winged warbler has white wing bars and a black eyeline.

66

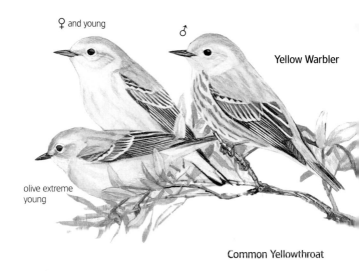

♀ and young

♂

Yellow Warbler

olive extreme
young

Common Yellowthroat

young ♂

♂

♀

WARBLERS

BLACK-AND-WHITE WARBLER

AMERICAN REDSTART

The male blackpoll warbler can be confused with the black-and-white, but it is a late spring migrant and is usually in the canopy, hidden by foliage.

Male blackpoll warblers have a solid black cap and less dramatic striping.

Black-and-white warblers are one of the earliest spring migrants. They are relatively easy to see because they arrive when trees are still bare. Like the nuthatches (p. 38), they scour the trunks and large limbs of trees for insects and larvae.

There is no yellow on the **black-and-white warbler,** and it has white wing bars. The black and white stripes on its head and body distinguish it from all other warblers. Note the black throat that distinguishes the male in spring. The male's throat is white in fall, but the patch around the eye remains black. It is grayish or lacking in females.

Redstarts are warblers, and the American redstart is one of the most beautiful. Latin America got it right when they named it *candelita,* or "little torch."

The salmon color on the male **American redstart** is replaced by yellow on the female. The patches in the wings are not wing bars. Wing bars are nearer the shoulder of a bird, not on the flight feathers themselves. When feeding in a shrub or tree, the American redstart is very active, flashing the bright colors in its wings and tail. It is often seen chasing flying bugs in short, wild flights.

Black-and-white Warbler

♀

spring ♂

☿

American Redstart

♂

CHICKADEES AND TITMOUSE

TUFTED TITMOUSE

CAROLINA CHICKADEE

BLACK-CAPPED CHICKADEE

The rise that the artist, Larry McQueen, shows on the hind neck of the black-capped may look unusual but is often displayed. Check for it on your chickadees.

Some of the boldest and also most welcome birds at backyard feeders are the chickadees and the tufted titmouse. The birds are closely related and have similar habits. During the summer, they feed mostly on insects and visit feeders infrequently. In winter, they regularly attend backyard feeders to eat seeds, nuts, and suet.

A perky crest and buff flanks distinguish the **tufted titmouse.**

Whether you see the **Carolina chickadee** or the **black-capped chickadee** depends upon where your backyard is. There is only a narrow band where the ranges of the two birds overlap, and in that band there are some hybrids.

The chickadees can be separated by a subtle but noticeable plumage mark. Check the wings. The Carolina chickadee can show some white or pale streaking on the folded wing, but the black-capped has distinct white in the folded wing and forming a bar on the shoulder. Black-caps have a four-syllable song, *fee-bee, fee-bay.* Carolinas give two or three notes, *fee-bee* or *fee-bee-ee.* The call of both birds is the same: a clear, scolding *chick-a-dee-dee-dee,* given slightly faster and higher-pitched by the Carolina chickadee.

Tufted Titmouse

Carolina Chickadee

Black-capped Chickadee

KINGLETS AND GNATCATCHER

RUBY-CROWNED KINGLET

GOLDEN-CROWNED KINGLET

BLUE-GRAY GNATCATCHER

The tiny kinglets and gnatcatchers are closely related in spite of their different shapes. Kinglets nest in northern conifers and are usually seen in eastern parks in migration and winter. They occasionally visit backyard shrubs and trees but not feeders. The ruby-crowned kinglet takes a few seeds in winter, but all kinglets manage to find hidden larvae and insect matter even in cold and snowy weather.

The color of its crown and the white eyebrow are good marks for the **golden-crowned kinglet. Ruby-crowned kinglets** are more nondescript; only the male shows red, and it is usually concealed. The tiny bill, plump body, and short tail give the ruby-crowned a different look from the warblers it might be confused with. The clinching marks are a white eye-ring broken at the top and a white wing bar bordered below by a dark patch — the kinglet patch.

The **blue-gray gnatcatcher** is the only tiny, slim bird with a long tail likely to be seen in eastern backyards. It is very fidgety, often cocking its tail expressively and flashing the white underside. Both sexes have a white eye-ring; males have a narrow black eyebrow and a blue-gray crown. Gnatcatchers feed on bugs, picking them from leaves and from the air, often in the crown of a shade tree.

Ruby-crowned Kinglet

♀

♂

Golden-crowned Kinglet

♀

♂

Blue-gray Gnatcatcher

♀

summer ♂

CARDINAL AND TOWHEE

CARDINAL

EASTERN TOWHEE

Widely known as the rufous-sided towhee, the eastern towhee got its new name in 1995 when it was determined to be a separate species from similar birds in the West.

Often the first to arrive at a backyard feeder in the morning and the last to stop by for a snack before dark, cardinals are the main reason many people have backyard feeders. The cardinal's range has steadily expanded northward because of the availability of sunflower seeds at feeders, allowing them to overwinter.

Even the brownish female **cardinal** is easily recognized by its crest, the red in its wings and tail, and its heavy conical bill. Young birds look like females but have dull bills instead of the bright orange-red bills of females.

The eastern towhee is declining at a faster rate than any other bird in the East. Like the brown thrasher (p. 44) and wood thrush (p. 56), it feeds in ground litter and is almost always hidden in shadows and shrubs. Parks and roadsides can provide good habitat, and so can a brushy backyard area.

The rusty-colored sides are good marks for adult **eastern towhees.** Males have black hoods and backs; females, brown. Long black tails with white in the corners are prominent marks for both the adults and the streaked, brown young birds. Their song, a distinctive *drink-your-tea,* or their namesake *tow-hee* call is often the best clue to the bird's presence.

74

♀

♂

Cardinal

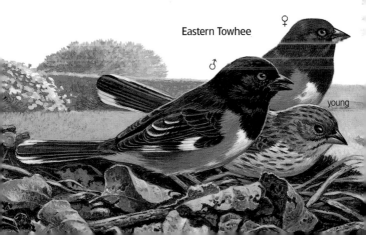

Eastern Towhee

♀

♂

young

GROSBEAKS

ROSE-BREASTED GROSBEAK

EVENING GROSBEAK

Pine grosbeaks are occasional winter visitors from the north to as far south as Pennsylvania and New Jersey. They flock like evening grosbeaks, but the male is red with white wing bars; the female, gray with an olive head and rump.

Big finches with very heavy bills, the grosbeaks are special visitors to back-yard feeders. Rose-breasted grosbeaks usually visit only in spring and are often seen in pairs. Evening grosbeaks gather in wandering flocks and show up at feeders in winter.

Rose-breasted grosbeaks eat insects as much as seeds in summer, so they are seldom regular visitors to a sunflower seed station. In spring, adult male **rose-breasted grosbeaks** are impressively beautiful and easy to identify. In fall, they look a lot like females but keep their black wings and tail and a rose blush on their breasts.

The female has striped underparts like many smaller finches. The large bill and distinct head stripes are her best marks. Young birds in fall resemble the female; young males have buff breasts. Males of all ages have red underwings; females, yellow.

The male **evening grosbeak** wears the same color plumage all year. The large white wing patches, stubby tail, and yellow forehead and eyebrows are all easily seen marks. Females are much grayer and have smaller white wing patches. Evening grosbeaks are attracted by road salt as well as sunflower seeds. They are relatively tame birds that move deliberately.

76

young fall ♂

♀ ♂

Rose-breasted
Grosbeak

Evening Grosbeak

♂

♀

FINCHES AND BUNTING

AMERICAN GOLDFINCH

PINE SISKIN

INDIGO BUNTING

Goldfinches are easily attracted to backyards by thistle seed feeders. Indigo buntings are summer visitors and are much rarer in backyards, preferring the scrubby growth of roadsides and fencerows. Pine siskins visit in winter, irregularly.

Although the male **American goldfinch** in summer plumage is easily recognized, female and fall birds are a dull, unstreaked olive brown above. Their white undertails are good marks. Males in winter resemble females but retain their black wings and tail and a small, bright yellow shoulder patch.

Pine siskins have a sharply pointed bill for a finch — a small mark, but a good one, separating them from other brown striped finches. The yellow, mostly in the wings, is not obvious.

Only the male **indigo bunting** in spring and summer is an iridescent indigo blue, and in shadow it often looks black. The female and young are dull brown with vague streaking on their breasts. Some can show a flash of blue in their wings and tail or a pale blue wash on the rump and shoulder. Brown birds with patches of bright blue plumage are males, either adults in fall, molting to their brown winter plumage, or yearlings in spring that are still acquiring the full breeding plumage.

Blue grosbeaks are much like indigo buntings. The blue grosbeak is an inch or two larger and has a heavier bill and rusty-brown wing bars.

78

American Goldfinch

winter

summer ♂

summer ♀

Pine Siskin

American goldfinch

pine siskin

yearling ♂

spring ♂

fall ♂

Indigo Bunting

♀

RED FINCHES

HOUSE FINCH

PURPLE FINCH

An Arctic finch, the common redpoll, sometimes invades the northern states in winter in large flocks. It resembles a small female house finch but has a well-defined patch of red on the forehead and some black around the bill.

Both house and purple finches are seen in backyards, often in the same backyard. It wasn't always so. House finches are a western species introduced in Long Island, New York, in the 1940s. They have proliferated, partly at the expense of the purple finch.

Males of both species have a splash of red that varies considerably among individuals. Separating the two species requires care. The females are plain, brown-striped birds that require even more care in identification.

House finches are a little slimmer than **purple finches** and have smaller heads and bills. Side by side the difference is perceptible. The best mark for male house finch is the distinct brown streaking on its sides and belly. Purple finches have blurry, reddish side streaks at most. The red on the male house finch's head is concentrated on the forehead and eyebrows. On the purple finch, the red extends onto the crown, nape, and back and tends to be more wine-colored.

The contrast of the broad white eyebrow and whisker stripe on the female purple finch is her best mark. The face of the female house finch is much plainer; her breast streaks are a bit finer and extend all the way under her less deeply notched tail.

House Finch

♀

♂

Purple Finch

♂

♀

JUNCO AND SPARROW

DARK-EYED JUNCO

HOUSE SPARROW

Snow bird is one of the popular and very appropriate names for the junco. When the weather turns cold and snow is forecast, the juncos return. The house sparrow has also inspired many popular names, including English sparrow and feathered rat.

Eastern juncos look different from western ones. Scientists have often reversed themselves on whether juncos in the East are a separate species (the slate-colored junco) or a race of the dark-eyed junco. Currently they are considered a race.

Call them what you will, **juncos** in the East are easy to identify. The white outer tail feathers and white belly contrast conspicuously with the slate gray back and hood. Also note the pale bill. Females are duller, browner, and can show contrast between the hood and the back.

House sparrows were introduced to New York from Europe in 1851. After years of expanding their range and numbers, they now inhabit neighborhoods and farms (but not wild areas) throughout the United States. They are beginning to decline, although perhaps not at your feeder. Male **house sparrows** have a black bib and chestnut head markings. The female is best identified by the combination of plain underparts, pale eyebrow, and pale bill.

♀

♂ Dark-eyed Junco

fall ♂

♀ House Sparrow

♂

CROWNED SPARROWS

WHITE-THROATED SPARROW

WHITE-CROWNED SPARROW

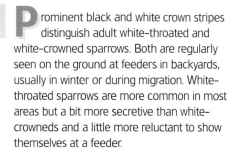

Prominent black and white crown stripes distinguish adult white-throated and white-crowned sparrows. Both are regularly seen on the ground at feeders in backyards, usually in winter or during migration. White-throated sparrows are more common in most areas but a bit more secretive than white-crowneds and a little more reluctant to show themselves at a feeder.

White-throated and white-crowned sparrows are both a little larger than most sparrows. The best mark for the **white-crowned sparrow** (after the black-and-white crown of the adult) is the dull pinkish bill. "Gambell's" is a western form that has white in front of the eye, not black as in eastern birds.

The **white-throated sparrow** has a white throat, and most have a spot of yellow in front of the eye. It also seems to have little or no neck; the head sits squarely on the shoulders, while the white-crowned shows more neck.

Heads of both species can be striped in shades of brown instead of black and white. Brown stripes on a white-crowned sparrow are the mark of a young bird. On a white-throated, brown stripes are also worn by some adults. Very young birds of both species have brown streaks on their breasts.

very young
late summer

White-throated Sparrow

tan-striped
form

very young
late summer

young

White-crowned Sparrow

Gambell's
form

RUSTY CAPPED SPARROWS

TREE SPARROW

FIELD SPARROW

CHIPPING SPARROW

The swamp sparrow resembles a chipping sparrow in winter. It is a shy wetland bird with a long rounded, not notched, tail and no dark eyeline.

The tree sparrow and the chipping sparrow are both regular backyard birds. Chipping sparrows like front lawns and unpaved driveways as well or better. Field sparrows are shy birds, more likely seen in the brush or briars of a park or nature center.

Not all plumages of these closely related, small, slim sparrows show a rusty cap or crown stripes, but most do. All three have fairly long, notched tails, and all flock in winter. (Tail shape is a good clue for identifying small brown sparrows.) The **tree sparrow** is a winter visitor with a prominent "stickpin" on its plain breast.

Best marks for the **field sparrow** are its bright pink bill and the white eye-ring. The eye-ring on the relatively plain face gives the bird a blank look.

Chipping sparrows have a bright rusty crown in summer, bordered by a white eyebrow and a black eyeline that extends all the way to the bill. They are summer visitors over much of the East, replacing the tree sparrows that migrate to the Arctic to nest. The face and crown are duller in winter, especially in first-winter birds. The black eyeline is not as bold in winter but still extends in front of the eye.

Tree Sparrow

very young
late summer

Field Sparrow

very young
late summer

Chipping Sparrow

very young
late summer

1st winter

summer

STREAKED SPARROWS

SONG SPARROW

SAVANNAH SPARROW

FOX SPARROW

The savannah sparrow has several color variations, including a very pale form known as the Ipswich sparrow that winters on coastal dunes in the Northeast.

Brown streaking on the breast is an important mark for song, savannah, and fox sparrows. Although clear-breasted sparrows show breast streaks when they are young, most streaks are lost soon after they leave the nest.

Not all birds with streaked breasts are sparrows, however. See the brown thrasher (p. 44), the female red-winged blackbird (p. 48), the young cowbird (p. 50), the pine siskin (p. 78), and the female finches (p. 80).

Song sparrows are common on the ground in backyards. The fox sparrow also visits backyards but is wary and reluctant to come out from cover. Like the brown thrasher (p. 44) and the eastern towhee (p. 74), it feeds in the ground litter under shrubs and brush. Savannah sparrows are seen in agricultural fields, grassy roadsides, and parks.

The center spot on the breast often used to identify **song sparrows** is not a conclusive mark; fox sparrows have it and so do many savannahs. The song sparrow's heavy black whisker mark and long rounded tail should also be noted. **Savannah sparrows** have a short notched tail and usually a lighter whisker. Many have a yellow spot in front of the eye. The **fox sparrow** is a large rusty red bird with especially bright color on the tail and rump.

Song Sparrow

young

Savannah Sparrow

Fox Sparrow

Sooner or later all bird-watchers, even the most casual, wonder how many different species they have seen or how many have visited their backyards. Keeping a record is the only way to know. A list of species seen can become part of the pleasure of bird-watching.

Your backyard list can be put to scientific use by the Cornell Lab of Ornithology. Their Project FeederWatch, begun in 1987 as a joint US-Canadian project with Bird Studies Canada, compiles the counts of backyard birders. Participants receive a research kit and a quarterly newsletter of feeder-watch results for a low annual fee. For more information, call 1-800-843-2473 (1-519-586-3531 in Canada).

✓ Species		Date	Location
◯ RED-WINGED **B**LACKBIRD *Agelaius phoeniceus*[1]	48	....	....
◯ EASTERN **B**LUEBIRD *Sialia sialis*	58	....	....
◯ **B**OBWHITE Northern Bobwhite[2] *Colinus virginianus*	30	....	....
◯ INDIGO **B**UNTING *Passerina cyanea*	78	....	....
◯ **C**ARDINAL Northern Cardinal *Cardinalis cardinalis*	74	....	....
◯ **C**ATBIRD Gray Catbird *Dumetella carolinensis*	58	....	....

[1] Names in *italics* are the scientific names adopted by the American Ornithologists' Union.
[2] When the AOU English name differs from the common name used in this guide, the official AOU English name is given on the second line.

✓ Species	Date	Location

○ BLACK-CAPPED **C**HICKADEE 70
Parus atricapillus

○ CAROLINA **C**HICKADEE 70
Parus carolinensis

○ BROWN-HEADED **C**OWBIRD 50
Molothrus ater

○ BROWN **C**REEPER 38
Certhia americana

○ AMERICAN **C**ROW 46
Corvus brachyrhynchos

○ FISH **C**ROW 46
Corvus ossifragus

○ MOURNING **D**OVE 32
Zenaida macroura

○ ROCK **D**OVE 32
Columba livia

COMMON GROUND-DOVE
*see **G**ROUND-DOVE*

○ HOUSE **F**INCH 80
Carpodacus mexicanus

○ PURPLE **F**INCH 80
Carpodacus purpureus

○ YELLOW-SHAFTED **F**LICKER 36
Northern Flicker
Colaptes auratus

○ GREAT CRESTED **F**LYCATCHER 42
Myiarchus crinitus

○ BLUE-GRAY **G**NATCATCHER 72
Polioptila caerulea

○ AMERICAN **G**OLDFINCH 78
Carduelis tristis

○ COMMON **G**RACKLE 46
Quiscalus quiscula

○ EVENING **G**ROSBEAK 76
Coccothraustes vespertinus

✓ Species	Date	Location

○ ROSE-BREASTED **G**ROSBEAK 76
Pheucticus ludovicianus

○ COMMON **G**ROUND-DOVE 32
Columbina passerina

○ COOPER'S **H**AWK 24
Accipiter cooperii

○ RED-TAILED **H**AWK 22
Buteo jamaicensis

○ SHARP-SHINNED **H**AWK 24
Accipiter striatus

○ RUBY-THROATED **H**UMMINGBIRD 28
Archilochus colubris

○ BLUE **J**AY 48
Cyanocitta cristata

○ DARK-EYED **J**UNCO 82
Junco hyemalis

○ **K**ESTREL 22
American Kestrel
Falco sparverius

○ EASTERN **K**INGBIRD 40
Tyrannus tyrannus

○ GOLDEN-CROWNED **K**INGLET 72
Regulus satrapa

○ RUBY-CROWNED **K**INGLET 72
Regulus calendula

○ PURPLE **M**ARTIN 26
Progne subis

○ EASTERN **M**EADOWLARK 54
Sturnella magna

○ **M**OCKINGBIRD 48
Northern Mockingbird
Mimus polyglottos

○ COMMON **N**IGHTHAWK 18
Chordeiles minor

✓ **Species**	**Date**	**Location**
⃝ RED-BREASTED **N**UTHATCH 38 *Sitta canadensis*	....	....
⃝ WHITE-BREASTED **N**UTHATCH 38 *Sitta carolinensis*	....	....
⃝ BALTIMORE **O**RIOLE 52 *Icterus galbula*	....	....
⃝ ORCHARD **O**RIOLE 52 *Icterus spurius*	....	....
⃝ BARN **O**WL 18 *Tyto alba*	....	....
EASTERN SCREECH-OWL see **S**CREECH-OWL	....	....
⃝ RING-NECKED **P**HEASANT 30 *Phasianus colchicus*	....	....
⃝ EASTERN **P**HOEBE 42 *Sayornis phoebe*	....	....
PIGEON see ROCK **D**OVE	....	....
⃝ AMERICAN **R**EDSTART 68 *Setophaga ruticilla*	....	....
⃝ **R**OBIN 56 American Robin *Turdus migratorius*	....	....
⃝ EASTERN **S**CREECH-OWL 18 *Otus asio*	....	....
⃝ CHIPPING **S**PARROW 86 *Spizella passerina*	....	....
⃝ FIELD **S**PARROW 86 *Spizella pusilla*	....	....
⃝ FOX **S**PARROW 88 *Passerella iliaca*	....	....
⃝ HOUSE **S**PARROW 82 *Passer domesticus*	....	....

✓ Species	Date	Location

○ SAVANNAH **S**PARROW 88
  Passerculus sandwichensis

○ SONG **S**PARROW 88
  Melospiza melodia

○ TREE **S**PARROW 86
  American Tree Sparrow
  Spizella arborea

○ WHITE-CROWNED **S**PARROW 84
  Zonotrichia leucophrys

○ WHITE-THROATED **S**PARROW 84
  Zonotrichia albicollis

○ **S**TARLING 50
  European Starling
  Sturnus vulgaris

○ BARN **S**WALLOW 26
  Hirundo rustica

○ TREE **S**WALLOW 26
  Tachycineta bicolor

○ CHIMNEY **S**WIFT 28
  Chaetura pelagica

○ SCARLET **T**ANAGER 54
  Piranga olivacea

○ BROWN **T**HRASHER 44
  Toxostoma rufum

○ WOOD **T**HRUSH 56
  Hylocichla mustelina

○ TUFTED **T**ITMOUSE 70
  Parus bicolor

○ EASTERN **T**OWHEE 74
  Pipilo erythrophthalmus

○ BLUE-HEADED **V**IREO 60
  Vireo solitarius

○ RED-EYED **V**IREO 60
  Vireo olivaceus

✓ Species	Date	Location

○ WARBLING **V**IREO	60		
Vireo gilvus			
○ BLACK **V**ULTURE	20		
Coragyps atratus			
○ TURKEY **V**ULTURE	20		
Cathartes aura			
○ BLACK-AND-WHITE **W**ARBLER	68		
Mniotilta varia			
○ BLACK-THROATED GREEN **W**ARBLER	64		
Dendroica virens			
○ CHESTNUT-SIDED **W**ARBLER	62		
Dendroica pensylvanica			
○ MAGNOLIA **W**ARBLER	64		
Dendroica magnolia			
○ MYRTLE **W**ARBLER	62		
Yellow-rumped Warbler			
Dendroica coronata			
○ YELLOW **W**ARBLER	66		
Dendroica petechia			
○ CEDAR **W**AXWING	40		
Bombycilla cedrorum			
○ DOWNY **W**OODPECKER	34		
Picoides pubescens			
○ HAIRY **W**OODPECKER	34		
Picoides villosus			
○ RED-BELLIED **W**OODPECKER	36		
Melanerpes carolinus			
○ HOUSE **W**REN	44		
Troglodytes aedon			
○ WINTER **W**REN	44		
Troglodytes troglodytes			
○ COMMON **Y**ELLOWTHROAT	66		
Geothlypis trichas			

Want to Help Conserve Birds?

It's as Easy as ABC!

By becoming a member of the American
Bird Conservancy, you can help ensure
work is being done to protect many of the
species in this field guide. You can receive *Bird
Conservation* magazine quarterly to learn about bird
conservation throughout the Americas and *World Birdwatch*
magazine for information on international bird conservation.

Make a difference to birds.
Copy this card and mail to the address listed below.

☐ **Yes,** I want to become a member and receive *Bird
Conservation* magazine.
A check in the amount of $15 is enclosed.

☐ **Yes,** I want to become an International member of
ABC and receive both *Bird Conservation* and
World Birdwatch magazines.
A check in the amount of $40 is enclosed.

NAME

ADDRESS

CITY/STATE/ZIP CODE

Return to: American Bird Conservancy
1250 24th Street, NW; Suite 400; Washington, D.C. 20037
or call **1-888-BIRD-MAG** or e-mail: abc@abcbirds.org

Memberships are tax deductible to the extent allowable by law.